SALTA

TRAVEL

GUIDE

2024

JOAQUÍN CAMINO

Table of Contents

Introduction

Welcome to Salta

Nestled in the Lerma Valley at the foothills of the Andes, Salta is a city that captivates visitors with its rich history, vibrant culture, and stunning natural beauty. Known as "La Linda" or "The Beautiful," Salta offers a unique blend of colonial charm and indigenous traditions, making it one of Argentina's most enchanting destinations. From its well-preserved Spanish architecture to its lively plazas, this city is a treasure trove of experiences waiting to be explored. Whether you're a history enthusiast, an outdoor adventurer, or a culture lover, Salta promises an unforgettable journey that will leave you longing to return.

Why Visit Salta in 2024?

There has never been a better time to visit Salta than in 2024. The city is buzzing with new developments, cultural events, and the modern amenities that make it an ideal destination for travelers seeking both relaxation and adventure. In 2024, Salta will be hosting several major festivals, showcasing the best of its music, dance, and culinary traditions. The city's infrastructure has also seen significant improvements, with new hotels, restaurants, and transport options making it easier than ever to explore. Moreover, the surrounding region of Salta is experiencing a resurgence in eco-tourism, with new sustainable tours and activities that allow visitors to experience its breathtaking landscapes responsibly. From the iconic Train to the Clouds to the vineyards of Cafayate, Salta is a gateway to some of the most awe-inspiring natural wonders in South America. This guide will help you make the most of your visit, whether you're interested in trekking through the Andean foothills, sampling world-class wines, or delving into the city's rich cultural heritage.

How to Use This Guide

This guide is designed to be your comprehensive companion throughout your stay in Salta. Whether you're planning a weekend getaway or an extended exploration of the region, you'll find all the information you need within these pages. Each chapter is organized to provide you with practical advice, insider tips, and detailed descriptions of Salta's top attractions, accommodations, dining options, and activities. You'll also discover lesser-known gems that are off the beaten path, perfect for those looking to experience the city like a local. The guide begins with essential information on planning your trip, including the best times to visit, how to get to Salta, and what to pack. It then takes you through the city's vibrant neighborhoods, highlighting must-see sights, historical landmarks, and cultural institutions. Additionally, you'll find sections dedicated to outdoor adventures, dining and cuisine, arts and nightlife, shopping, and family-friendly activities. For those interested in sustainable travel, there's also a chapter on eco-friendly practices and responsible tourism. Use this guide as your roadmap to explore the beauty and diversity of Salta at your own pace.

Quick Facts About Salta

Before diving into your Salta adventure, here are a few quick facts to help you get acquainted with the city. Salta is the capital of the Salta Province in northwestern Argentina and has a population of approximately 620,000 people. The city sits at an elevation of 1,152 meters (3,780 feet) above sea level, giving it a pleasant climate year-round, with warm summers and mild winters. Salta is known for its colonial architecture, particularly in the historic city center, where you'll find beautifully preserved buildings such as the Cabildo and the Cathedral Basilica. The city is also a cultural hub, famous for its traditional folk music known as "zamba" and its vibrant festivals. The surrounding region is renowned for its dramatic landscapes, including the Calchaquí Valleys, Quebrada de Humahuaca, and the stunning salt flats of Salinas Grandes.

Additionally, Salta is part of Argentina's renowned wine country, with the nearby town of Cafayate producing some of the country's best Torrontés wines. These facts only scratch the surface of what makes Salta a unique and fascinating destination.

A Brief History of Salta

Salta's history is as rich and diverse as its landscapes. The region has been inhabited for thousands of years, with evidence of pre-Columbian civilizations such as the Diaguita and the Inca Empire, who left behind significant archaeological sites like the ruins of Tastil. The city of Salta was officially founded on April 16, 1582, by the Spanish conquistador Hernando de Lerma, who named it after the nearby valley. Salta quickly became an important colonial outpost due to its strategic location on the trade route between Lima and Buenos Aires. Throughout the colonial period, Salta prospered as a center for agriculture, trade, and culture, leaving a legacy of stunning Spanish architecture that still stands today. The city played a crucial role during Argentina's War of Independence, serving as a key battleground where local hero General Martín Miguel de Güemes led the gauchos in the fight against Spanish forces. This period of resistance is celebrated in Salta's many monuments and museums. In the centuries that followed, Salta continued to grow and evolve, becoming a melting pot of indigenous, Spanish, and immigrant cultures. Today, Salta is a vibrant, modern city that proudly preserves its historical heritage while embracing the future, making it a must-visit destination for anyone interested in Argentina's rich cultural tapestry.

Chapter 1

Getting to Salta

Salta, a captivating city in Argentina's northwest, is known for its colonial architecture, vibrant culture, and breathtaking natural landscapes. Planning your trip to Salta involves careful consideration of the best times to visit, understanding the available travel options, and navigating the city once you arrive. Here's a comprehensive guide to help you get to Salta and make the most of your stay.

Best Times to Visit

Salta enjoys a pleasant climate year-round, making it a great destination no matter when you choose to visit. However, the best times to visit are during the spring (September to November) and fall (March to May) when the weather is mild, and the landscapes are particularly stunning. During these periods, temperatures range between 15°C (59°F) and 25°C (77°F), making it ideal for outdoor activities and sightseeing. The springtime sees the countryside in full bloom, while autumn offers the golden hues of changing foliage.

The summer months (December to February) in Salta can be warm and humid, with temperatures sometimes soaring above 30°C (86°F). This season also brings occasional heavy rains, especially in January and February, which can affect travel plans, particularly in the surrounding rural areas. Conversely, winter (June to August) is cooler, with temperatures dipping to around 5°C (41°F) at night, but it is generally dry, making it a good time for exploring the city and nearby attractions without the crowds.

Flights to Salta

Traveling to Salta by air is the most convenient option for international and domestic travelers. Martín Miguel de Güemes International Airport

(SLA) is the main gateway to the region, located just 7 kilometers (4.3 miles) southwest of the city center. The airport serves several domestic flights from major cities across Argentina, including Buenos Aires, Córdoba, and Mendoza, as well as some international flights from neighboring countries.

For those flying from overseas, the most common route is to connect through Buenos Aires' Ministro Pistarini International Airport (EZE), also known as Ezeiza Airport. From there, you can take a domestic flight to Salta, which takes about two hours. Airlines such as Aerolíneas Argentinas, JetSMART, and Flybondi operate regular flights to Salta, offering multiple options throughout the day.

Upon arrival at Martín Miguel de Güemes International Airport, you can take a taxi or a shuttle bus to reach the city center. The journey takes around 20 minutes, depending on traffic. Taxis are readily available outside the terminal, and the fare is reasonable. Alternatively, some hotels offer airport transfer services, which can be arranged in advance.

Traveling by Bus or Car

For those who prefer to travel by land, Salta is well-connected by a network of buses and roads. Long-distance buses are a popular and cost-effective way to travel to Salta from other parts of Argentina. The city's bus terminal, Terminal de Ómnibus de Salta, is located near the city center and is served by numerous bus companies offering routes from Buenos Aires, Córdoba, Mendoza, and other major cities. The bus journey from Buenos Aires to Salta takes approximately 20 hours, with both daytime and overnight services available. Buses in Argentina are generally comfortable, with options ranging from standard seats to fully reclining "cama" seats, which provide a more luxurious travel experience.

Driving to Salta is another option, particularly if you enjoy road trips and want to explore the stunning landscapes of northern Argentina at your own pace. The most common route from Buenos Aires is via National Route 9, which covers a distance of approximately 1,600 kilometers (994 miles). The journey can take around 18 to 20 hours, depending on traffic and stops along the way. The roads are generally in good condition, but it's advisable to plan your route carefully and consider stopping overnight in a city like Córdoba or Tucumán to break up the long drive. Renting a car in Salta is also a great option for exploring the surrounding regions, such as the Quebrada de Humahuaca, Cafayate, and Cachi.

Getting Around the City

Once in Salta, getting around is relatively easy, thanks to the city's compact layout and efficient public transportation system. Most of the city's main attractions, such as the Plaza 9 de Julio, the Cathedral of Salta, and the Museo de Arqueología de Alta Montaña (MAAM), are located within walking distance of each other in the city center.

Walking is a pleasant way to explore the city, especially given its charming colonial architecture and lively streets.

For longer distances, Salta has a reliable bus network that covers most areas of the city and its outskirts. Buses are frequent and affordable, making them a convenient option for getting around. Tickets can be purchased at kiosks or paid for using a rechargeable SUBE card, which is also used in other major Argentine cities.

Taxis and ride-sharing services like Uber are widely available in Salta and provide a more flexible way to get around, especially if you prefer not to wait for a bus. Taxis are metered, and fares are reasonable, but it's always a good idea to confirm the estimated fare with the driver before starting your journey.

For those who prefer more independence, renting a car is a great option, especially if you plan to explore the surrounding areas or take day trips to nearby attractions. Several car rental agencies operate in Salta, both at the airport and in the city center. Having a car allows you to visit remote destinations like the Salinas Grandes or the wine region of Cafayate at your own pace.

Visa and Entry Requirements

Before traveling to Salta, it's essential to check the visa and entry requirements for Argentina, which vary depending on your nationality. Citizens of many countries, including the United States, Canada, the European Union, Australia, and New Zealand, do not require a visa for short stays of up to 90 days for tourism purposes. However, you must have a valid passport with at least six months of validity remaining from your planned date of entry.

If you are traveling from a country that requires a visa, you should apply for one at your nearest Argentine consulate before your trip. The visa application process typically requires you to submit a completed application form, a passport-sized photo, proof of onward travel, and proof of sufficient funds for your stay. Processing times can vary, so it's advisable to apply well in advance of your planned departure date.

Upon arrival in Argentina, you will need to complete an immigration form and present it, along with your passport, to the immigration authorities. You may also be asked to show proof of onward travel, such as a return ticket, and demonstrate that you have sufficient funds to cover your stay. Once cleared, you will receive an entry stamp in your passport, which indicates the date by which you must leave the country.

For those planning to stay longer than 90 days or to engage in activities beyond tourism, such as work or study, it is necessary to apply for the appropriate visa. Argentina also offers a reciprocity fee system for citizens of certain countries, including the United States and Canada, although this fee has been suspended at various times, so it's important to check the latest information before you travel.

With the practicalities of getting to Salta covered, you can focus on enjoying the rich cultural experiences, stunning landscapes, and warm hospitality that this unique region has to offer. Whether you arrive by air, bus, or car, Salta promises an unforgettable adventure in the heart of Argentina.

Chapter 2

Where to Stay in Salta

Salta, known for its colonial charm and vibrant culture, offers a diverse range of accommodation options that cater to different tastes and budgets. Whether you're drawn to the historical allure of the city center, the lively atmosphere of Balcarce, or the tranquil beauty of San Lorenzo, Salta's neighborhoods each offer a unique experience. Here's an in-depth look at the best places to stay during your visit to Salta.

Top Neighborhoods

Historic City Center: The heart of Salta, the Historic City Center, is where the city's rich history and cultural heritage are most palpable. Staying here places you within walking distance of iconic landmarks such as the Plaza 9 de Julio, the

Cathedral, and the MAAM (Museum of High Altitude Archaeology). The area is lined with colonial-era buildings, cobblestone streets, and charming plazas, offering a quintessentially Salteño experience. The convenience of being close to top attractions, restaurants, and shops makes the Historic City Center a favorite among tourists.

Balcarce District: For those who enjoy a vibrant nightlife and cultural scene, the Balcarce District is the place to be. This neighborhood is famous for its peñas, where you can enjoy traditional Argentine folk music and dancing. Balcarce Street is lined with restaurants, bars, and clubs, making it a lively area to stay in. The district is also home to the Train to the Clouds station, offering easy access to one of Salta's most famous excursions. The Balcarce District is perfect for travelers looking to immerse themselves in the local culture while enjoying a bustling atmosphere.

San Lorenzo: Just a short drive from the city center, San Lorenzo offers a peaceful retreat in a lush, green setting. Known for its natural beauty, San Lorenzo is surrounded by hills and forests, providing a tranquil environment ideal for relaxation. This area is popular among those seeking outdoor activities such as hiking, horseback riding, and birdwatching. San Lorenzo is also home to several charming boutique hotels and estancias, making it a great choice for nature lovers who want to stay close to the city while enjoying a more serene atmosphere.

Best Hotels

Salta boasts a selection of top-notch hotels that provide luxury and comfort with a touch of local charm. Among the best is the Hotel Alejandro I, located in the heart of the Historic City Center. This five-star hotel is known for its elegant rooms, excellent service, and amenities that include a spa, indoor pool, and gourmet restaurant. Another standout is Legado Mítico Salta, a boutique hotel housed in a restored colonial mansion. Each room in this hotel is uniquely themed, paying homage to prominent figures in Argentine history. The hotel's intimate setting and attention to detail make it a favorite among discerning travelers.

For a more modern experience, the Design Suites Salta offers sleek, contemporary accommodations with panoramic views of the city. Located just steps from Plaza 9 de Julio, this hotel combines modern design with luxurious comfort, featuring an on-site spa, restaurant, and rooftop pool. Sheraton Salta Hotel is another excellent option, especially for those seeking a more international hotel experience. Situated in the Monumento district, the hotel offers spacious rooms with breathtaking views of the Lerma Valley and a range of amenities including a large outdoor pool, fitness center, and several dining options.

Boutique Stays

Salta's boutique hotels provide a more intimate and personalized experience, often housed in beautifully restored historic buildings. Kkala Boutique Hotel in the Tres Cerritos neighborhood is a prime example, offering a luxurious yet cozy atmosphere with stunning views of the city. The hotel's decor blends modern comfort with traditional elements, and its terrace and outdoor pool are perfect for unwinding after a day of exploring.

Another boutique gem is Villa Vicuña, located in the heart of the city center. This charming hotel features elegant rooms adorned with antique furnishings and a tranquil courtyard garden. The personalized service and attention to detail make Villa Vicuña a top choice for travelers seeking a unique and memorable stay.

For those who prefer a countryside setting, House of Jasmines is an exquisite boutique estancia just outside Salta. Surrounded by lush gardens and with the Andes as a backdrop, this boutique stay offers an authentic Argentine experience with modern luxuries, including a spa, gourmet dining, and outdoor activities such as horseback riding.

Budget-Friendly Accommodations

Travelers on a budget will find plenty of affordable accommodation options in Salta without sacrificing comfort or convenience. Hotel Marilian is a popular budget choice located just a few blocks from Plaza 9 de Julio. The hotel offers simple, clean rooms with all the basic amenities, including free Wi-Fi and a complimentary breakfast. Its central location makes it an ideal base for exploring the city.

Hostal El Litoral is another budget-friendly option offering comfortable rooms in a homely environment. Located near Balcarce Street, this hostel is perfect for travelers who want to stay close to the action without breaking the bank. The friendly staff and cozy atmosphere make it a great choice for budget-conscious visitors.

For those who prefer a more social environment, Backpackers Hostel Salta offers dormitory-style accommodations as well as private rooms. The hostel is located near the city center and features a communal kitchen, a garden, and a bar, making it a great place to meet other travelers.

Unique Stays: Estancias and Haciendas

For a truly unique and authentic Argentine experience, consider staying at one of Salta's estancias or haciendas. These traditional country estates offer a glimpse into the region's rural life, with the added comforts of modern amenities.

Estancia El Bordo de las Lanzas is one of the oldest estancias in the region, dating back to the 1600s. Located about an hour from Salta, this historic estate offers guests the chance to experience traditional estancia life, including horseback riding, gaucho demonstrations, and farm tours. The estancia's beautifully preserved colonial architecture and tranquil setting provide a perfect escape from the hustle and bustle of city life.

Another exceptional option is Finca Valentina, a boutique estancia located just outside Salta. This charming property combines the rustic charm of a traditional estancia with the comforts of a luxury hotel. Guests can enjoy activities such as hiking, cooking classes, and wine tastings, all while taking in the stunning views of the surrounding mountains.

Estancia La Candelaria offers a more intimate experience, with only a few guest rooms available. This family-run estancia is known for its warm hospitality and personalized service. Guests can participate in daily farm activities or simply relax and enjoy the peaceful countryside.

Salta's diverse range of accommodations ensures that every traveler can find the perfect place to stay, whether you're seeking luxury, boutique charm, budget-friendly options, or a unique estancia experience. Each neighborhood and lodging option offers its own distinct flavor, allowing visitors to immerse themselves fully in the beauty and culture of this captivating region.

Chapter 3

Exploring Salta's History and Culture

Salta, a city steeped in history and rich in cultural heritage, offers visitors an opportunity to immerse themselves in the essence of northern Argentina. Exploring Salta's history and culture is a journey through time, where colonial architecture, indigenous traditions, and the spirit of the gaucho come alive in every corner of the city. This section will guide you through some of the most iconic landmarks and cultural experiences that define Salta.

At the heart of Salta lies Plaza 9 de Julio, the city's main square and a focal point for both locals and visitors. This vibrant plaza is surrounded by historic buildings, each telling a story of the city's colonial past. The square is a perfect starting point for exploring Salta, with its beautifully manicured gardens, fountains, and statues that invite you to pause and take in the atmosphere. Plaza 9 de Julio is more than just a public space; it is the living room of Salta, where locals gather for leisurely strolls, and street performers add to the lively ambiance. The square is also home to some of the city's most significant landmarks, making it a must-visit destination for anyone interested in Salta's history and culture.

One of the most striking buildings on Plaza 9 de Julio is the Cathedral Basilica of Salta. This magnificent cathedral, with its pink façade and twin bell towers, is an architectural gem that reflects the city's deep-rooted Catholic heritage. Constructed in the 19th century, the cathedral is a blend of neoclassical and baroque styles, with ornate altars, intricate carvings, and beautiful stained-glass windows. Inside, the atmosphere is one of reverence and tranquility, offering a space for reflection and prayer. The cathedral is also the final resting place of General Martín Miguel de Güemes, a national hero who played a crucial role in Argentina's fight for independence. Visiting the Cathedral Basilica of Salta is not only a spiritual experience but also an opportunity to delve into the historical and cultural identity of the region.

A short walk from the cathedral is the Museo de Arqueología de Alta Montaña (MAAM), a museum that offers a fascinating glimpse into the pre-Columbian history of the Andes. MAAM is renowned for its collection of Inca artifacts, including the world-famous "Children of Llullaillaco," three mummified children discovered at the summit of the Llullaillaco volcano. These well-preserved mummies provide invaluable insights into the rituals and beliefs of the Inca civilization. The museum's exhibits are thoughtfully curated, with detailed explanations in both Spanish and English, making it accessible to a wide audience. Through its displays, MAAM not only preserves the past but also honors the indigenous cultures that continue to shape Salta's identity today.

Opposite the cathedral, you will find the Cabildo de Salta, a former colonial government building that now houses the Historical Museum of the North. The Cabildo is one of the oldest and best-preserved colonial buildings in Argentina, with its distinctive white arcades and central courtyard. Inside, the museum's exhibits take you on a journey through the history of Salta and the surrounding region, from the pre-Hispanic era to the colonial period and beyond. The collection includes a wide range of artifacts, from indigenous pottery and colonial-era furniture to historical documents and paintings. The Cabildo's architecture itself is a testament to the city's colonial past, with its thick adobe walls and wooden beams providing a glimpse into the building techniques of the time. A visit to the Cabildo de Salta is an essential part of understanding the city's historical and cultural evolution.

Another iconic religious site in Salta is the San Francisco Church and Convent. This stunning church, with its towering red and gold bell tower, is one of the most photographed landmarks in the city. The church dates back to the 17th century and is a masterpiece of colonial architecture, with its ornate façade, grand altars, and exquisite frescoes. The interior of the church is equally impressive, with its high vaulted ceilings, intricate woodwork, and religious art that reflects the deep devotion of the local community. The adjacent convent, which is still home to a small number of Franciscan monks, adds to the spiritual atmosphere of the site. San Francisco Church and Convent is not only a place of worship but also a symbol of the enduring influence of the Catholic Church in the cultural life of Salta.

No exploration of Salta's culture would be complete without acknowledging the Gaucho culture, which is deeply ingrained in the identity of the region. The gauchos, the skilled horsemen and cowboys of the Argentine pampas, are celebrated as symbols of freedom, bravery, and independence. In Salta, gaucho culture is alive and well, with traditional festivals, rodeos, and folk music that honor their way of life. One of the most important events in the gaucho calendar is the annual Güemes Day, held in June to commemorate the death of General Martín Miguel de Güemes. During this festival, gauchos from all over the region gather in Salta to participate in parades, horse riding competitions, and cultural performances. It is a vibrant and colorful celebration that offers a unique insight into the traditions and values of the gaucho community.

Exploring Salta's history and culture is a rich and rewarding experience that offers a deep understanding of the city's past and present. From the historic landmarks around Plaza 9 de Julio to the enduring traditions of the gauchos, Salta is a city that proudly showcases its cultural heritage while inviting visitors to become part of its story.

Chapter 4

Salta's Natural Wonders

Salta, often referred to as "La Linda" (The Beautiful), is a region blessed with an astonishing diversity of natural landscapes. From the towering Andes to the expansive salt flats, the natural wonders of Salta are as varied as they are breathtaking. Exploring these landscapes offers an unparalleled experience for nature lovers and adventurers alike, revealing the raw beauty of northern Argentina.

The journey through Salta's natural wonders begins with the Andes, the majestic mountain range that forms a dramatic backdrop to the region. The Andes are not just a geographical feature but a defining element of Salta's identity. As you venture into the mountains, you'll encounter landscapes that range from lush valleys to rugged peaks, each offering a unique perspective on the natural beauty of the area. The Andean region is also rich in cultural heritage, with small villages dotting the landscape, where indigenous traditions are still very much alive. The journey through the Andes is both a physical and spiritual experience, where the sheer scale of the mountains and the serenity of the environment create a profound connection with nature.

One of the most captivating day trips from Salta is to the Quebrada de Humahuaca, a UNESCO World Heritage site that stretches for 155 kilometers through the Jujuy Province. This spectacular valley, carved by the Río Grande, is renowned for its multicolored hills, which create a stunning contrast against the blue sky. The Quebrada de Humahuaca is not only a natural wonder but also a cultural treasure, with a history that dates back over 10,000 years. The valley was once a major trade route for indigenous peoples, and today it is home to a number of traditional villages, where you can witness the rich cultural heritage of the Andean communities. The landscapes of the Quebrada de Humahuaca are both surreal and awe-inspiring, offering a glimpse into a world where nature and culture are deeply intertwined.

Further south, the Cafayate and the Calchaquí Valley offer a different but equally stunning natural experience. The Calchaquí Valley is famous for its dramatic landscapes, characterized by rugged mountains, deep gorges, and vibrant red rock formations. The region is also one of Argentina's premier wine-producing areas, with Cafayate being the heart of the wine country. As you drive through the valley, you'll encounter vast vineyards that stretch as far as the eye can see, framed by the towering peaks of the Andes. The unique combination of altitude, climate, and soil in this region produces some of the best wines in Argentina, particularly the Torrontés, a fragrant white wine that has become the signature of Cafayate. Beyond the vineyards, the Calchaquí

Valley is home to natural wonders such as the Quebrada de las Conchas, where wind and water have sculpted the rocks into fantastical shapes, creating a landscape that feels almost otherworldly.

Another must-visit natural wonder in Salta is the Salinas Grandes, Argentina's great salt flats. Located on the border between Salta and Jujuy provinces, the Salinas Grandes are one of the largest salt flats in the world, covering an area of over 3,200 square kilometers. The salt flats are a stark, dazzling expanse of white that stretches to the horizon, creating a surreal and mesmerizing landscape. Walking on the salt flats is a unique experience, as the flat, reflective surface seems to blend seamlessly with the sky, creating the illusion of an infinite mirror. The Salinas Grandes are also an important part of the local economy, with salt being harvested by traditional methods that have been passed down through generations. Visiting the Salinas Grandes offers a rare opportunity to witness one of nature's most striking phenomena and to learn about the cultural and economic significance of this extraordinary landscape.

Back in the city of Salta, Cerro San Bernardo provides an opportunity to take in panoramic views of the city and the surrounding landscape. The hill is a popular spot for both locals and visitors, offering a peaceful retreat from the hustle and bustle of the city. You can reach the summit of Cerro San Bernardo by hiking up a series of well-maintained trails, or by taking a cable car that offers stunning views as you ascend. At the top, you'll be rewarded with breathtaking vistas of Salta, with the city's colonial architecture nestled against the backdrop of the Andes. The summit is also home to a beautifully landscaped park, with fountains, sculptures, and shaded areas where you can relax and enjoy the view. Cerro San Bernardo is not just a place to admire the scenery, but also a reminder of the close connection between the city and the natural landscape that surrounds it.

Salta's natural wonders offer a diverse and unforgettable experience for those who seek to explore the beauty of northern Argentina. From the towering peaks of the Andes to the vast expanses of the Salinas Grandes, each landscape tells its own story, reflecting the unique geological and cultural history of the region. Whether you're trekking through the mountains, exploring ancient valleys, or marveling at the otherworldly salt flats, Salta's natural wonders will leave you with memories that will last a lifetime.

Chapter 5

Outdoor Adventures in Salta

Salta is a paradise for outdoor enthusiasts, offering a wide range of activities that allow visitors to immerse themselves in the region's stunning natural landscapes. The combination of diverse terrains, from towering mountains to expansive valleys, makes Salta an ideal destination for those seeking adventure in the great outdoors. Whether you prefer the thrill of mountain biking or the serenity of a nature walk, Salta has something for everyone.

For those who love to explore on foot, Salta offers a variety of hiking trails and nature walks that showcase the region's natural beauty. The trails range from easy, leisurely walks through scenic valleys to more challenging hikes that take you deep into the Andean mountains. One of the most popular hiking destinations is the Quebrada de San Lorenzo, located just a short drive from the city of Salta. This lush, green valley is crisscrossed with trails that lead through dense forests, past cascading waterfalls, and up to viewpoints that offer breathtaking panoramas of the surrounding landscape. For those seeking a more challenging hike, the trails in the Calchaquí Valley provide an opportunity to explore rugged terrains and discover hidden gems, such as ancient rock formations and remote villages. Hiking in Salta is not just about physical activity; it's also a chance to connect with nature, breathe in the fresh mountain air, and experience the tranquility of the wilderness.

For adrenaline seekers, Salta's mountain biking routes offer an exhilarating way to explore the region's diverse landscapes. The rugged terrain of the Andes and the surrounding valleys provide a perfect playground for mountain bikers of all levels. Whether you're a seasoned rider or a beginner, you'll find trails that suit your skill level, from smooth, flowing paths to technical, rocky descents. One of the most popular routes is the Cuesta del Obispo, a winding road that climbs from the Lerma Valley to the high-altitude plains of the Parque Nacional Los Cardones. The route offers a mix of challenging climbs and thrilling descents, with stunning views of the valley below and the mountains beyond. For those looking for a more relaxed ride, the trails around the town of Cafayate offer a mix of scenic routes through vineyards and rolling hills. Mountain biking in Salta is a fantastic way to cover more ground and experience the region's natural beauty from a different perspective.

Another quintessential Salta experience is horseback riding in the valleys, a traditional activity that allows you to explore the landscape at a leisurely pace. Horseback riding is deeply rooted in the culture of the region, and there are numerous estancias (ranches) that offer guided rides through some of the most picturesque areas in Salta. Whether you're an experienced rider or a novice, you'll find that riding through the valleys on horseback provides a unique and intimate connection with the landscape. One of the most popular areas for horseback riding is the Lerma Valley, where you can ride through lush green pastures, along the banks of the Río Rosario, and up into the foothills of the Andes. The experience is made even more special by the opportunity to learn about the gaucho way of life, as many of the guides are local cowboys who share their knowledge of the land and their passion for horses. Horseback riding in Salta is not just an adventure; it's also a journey into the heart of the region's culture and traditions.

For those who crave the ultimate thrill, paragliding over the Andes offers an unforgettable adventure that combines adrenaline with awe-inspiring views. Salta's mountainous terrain provides the perfect conditions for paragliding, with reliable thermals and breathtaking landscapes that stretch out beneath you. The most popular spot for paragliding is Cerro San Bernardo, located just outside the city of Salta.

After a short hike to the launch site, you'll take off and soar high above the mountains, with the city of Salta and the surrounding valleys spread out below. The sensation of floating through the air, with the wind in your face and the vastness of the Andes all around you, is both exhilarating and serene. Paragliding in Salta is an experience that will leave you with a profound sense of freedom and a new appreciation for the natural beauty of the region.

Finally, exploring the Lerma Valley offers a more relaxed but equally rewarding outdoor adventure. The Lerma Valley, which stretches out to the south of the city of Salta, is a fertile region known for its agricultural production and picturesque landscapes. The valley is crisscrossed with rivers, dotted with small villages, and surrounded by rolling hills that provide a stunning backdrop for outdoor activities. Whether you choose to explore the valley on foot, by bike, or on horseback, you'll find that the Lerma Valley is a place of quiet beauty and rural charm. The valley is also home to several nature reserves and parks, where you can observe the local flora and fauna, including a wide variety of bird species. Exploring the Lerma Valley is a chance to experience the slower, more peaceful side of Salta, where the rhythms of rural life and the beauty of the natural landscape combine to create a truly special experience.

Salta offers a wealth of outdoor adventures that cater to all tastes and levels of experience. Whether you're hiking through pristine valleys, biking down rugged mountain trails, or soaring high above the Andes, the region's natural beauty and diverse landscapes provide the perfect setting for unforgettable experiences. Salta's outdoor adventures are not just about pushing your limits; they're also about discovering the unique connection between the land and its people, and experiencing the profound sense of wonder that comes from being immersed in nature.

Chapter 6

Dining and Cuisine

Salta is not only a feast for the eyes with its stunning landscapes but also a paradise for the palate. The region's culinary scene is deeply rooted in tradition, blending indigenous ingredients with Spanish influences to create a unique and flavorful cuisine. Dining in Salta is an experience that allows you to savor the rich cultural heritage of northern Argentina, with each dish telling a story of the land and its people.

At the heart of Salta's culinary identity are the traditional Salteño dishes, which have been passed down through generations. Among these, the empanadas salteñas are perhaps the most iconic. These savory pastries are a staple of Salteño cuisine, known for their delicate, flaky dough and flavorful fillings. Unlike empanadas from other regions of Argentina, which often feature a variety of meats and spices, Salteño empanadas are typically filled with finely chopped beef or chicken, potatoes, green onions, and a touch of cumin, all cooked to perfection. The secret to their distinctive taste lies in the cooking method, as they are traditionally baked in a clay oven, which imparts a unique, smoky flavor. Empanadas are a must-try for anyone visiting Salta, and they are often enjoyed as a snack or a light meal, accompanied by a glass of local wine or a cold beer.

Another cornerstone of Salteño cuisine is locro and humita, two traditional dishes that reflect the region's indigenous roots. Locro is a hearty stew made from corn, beans, potatoes, and a variety of meats, including pork, chorizo, and beef. It is typically slow-cooked for hours, allowing the flavors to meld together into a rich and satisfying dish. Locro is especially popular during the winter months and on national holidays, when it is often served as part of a communal meal. Humita, on the other hand, is a dish made from fresh corn that is ground into a paste and mixed with cheese, onions, and spices. The mixture is then wrapped in corn husks and steamed or boiled until cooked. Humita can be served as a side dish or as a main course, and its creamy texture and sweet, earthy flavor make it a favorite among locals and visitors alike.

No discussion of Argentine cuisine would be complete without mentioning the asado, or Argentine BBQ. Asado is more than just a meal in Salta; it is a social event, a time for family and friends to come together and enjoy good food and company. The asado typically features a variety of meats, including beef, pork, chicken, and sausages, all cooked over an open flame or on a grill. The meat is seasoned simply with salt and sometimes brushed with chimichurri, a tangy sauce made from parsley, garlic, vinegar, and oil. The result is meat that is tender, juicy, and full of flavor. Asado is often accompanied by side dishes such as grilled vegetables, salads, and bread, and it is usually paired with a robust red wine from the region. Experiencing an asado in Salta is a must for anyone who wants to understand the Argentine way of life and the importance of food in bringing people together.

For those looking to experience the best of Salta's culinary offerings, there are numerous restaurants in Salta that showcase the region's traditional flavors while also offering modern interpretations of classic dishes. One of the top dining destinations in the city is Doña Salta, a restaurant known for its authentic Salteño cuisine and warm, rustic ambiance. Here, you can sample a variety of regional specialties, including empanadas, locro, and tamales, all prepared with locally sourced ingredients. Another popular spot is El Solar del Convento, which offers a more upscale dining experience with a focus on Argentine beef and gourmet interpretations of traditional dishes. For those seeking a more contemporary take on Salteño cuisine, Ma Cuisine is a French-inspired restaurant that blends local ingredients with international techniques, resulting in dishes that are both innovative and deeply rooted in the region's culinary traditions.

Salta is also renowned for its local wineries and wine tasting experiences in Cafayate, a town located in the Calchaquí Valley that is considered the heart of Argentina's northern wine country. Cafayate's unique climate, characterized by high altitude, low humidity, and a wide temperature range, creates the perfect conditions for growing grapes, particularly the Torrontés variety, which is the region's signature white wine. Visitors to Cafayate can explore the many vineyards and wineries that dot the landscape, each offering tours and tastings that provide insight into the winemaking process and the distinctive characteristics of the local wines. Some of the most notable wineries in the area include Bodega El Esteco, a historic estate known for its elegant wines and stunning architecture, and Bodega Nanni, a family-owned winery that specializes in organic and biodynamic wines. Wine tasting in Cafayate is an unforgettable experience that allows you to savor the flavors of the region while taking in the breathtaking scenery of the valley.

For those who prefer a more casual dining experience, Salta's street food and local markets offer a wealth of options that are both delicious and affordable. Street vendors can be found throughout the city, serving up a variety of traditional snacks, from empanadas to choripán (a type of sausage sandwich) to tamales. These quick bites are perfect for enjoying on the go or while exploring the city's many attractions. The local markets, such as Mercado San Miguel, are also great places to sample Salteño cuisine and discover fresh, locally grown produce, artisanal cheeses, cured meats, and traditional sweets. The markets are bustling hubs of activity, where you can interact with local vendors and learn more about the ingredients that make Salta's cuisine so special.

While Salta is known for its meat-centric dishes, the city also offers a growing number of vegetarian and vegan options that cater to different dietary preferences. Many restaurants in Salta are beginning to incorporate plant-based dishes into their menus, using the region's abundant fresh produce to create flavorful and satisfying meals. For example, Chirimoya is a popular vegetarian restaurant that offers a variety of creative dishes made from locally sourced ingredients, including salads, veggie empanadas, and quinoa-based entrees. Another option is La Casona del Molino, which, while primarily known for its traditional Argentine fare, also offers vegetarian versions of classic dishes, such as humita and grilled vegetables. Whether you follow a plant-based diet or simply want to explore a different side of Salteño cuisine, you'll find plenty of delicious options that highlight the region's rich culinary diversity.

Dining in Salta is a journey through the flavors and traditions of northern Argentina. From the savory empanadas and hearty stews to the sweet, fragrant wines of Cafayate, the region's cuisine is a reflection of its diverse cultural heritage and the bounty of its land. Whether you're enjoying a traditional asado with friends, sampling street food at a local market, or exploring the innovative menus of Salta's best restaurants, you'll find that each meal in Salta is an opportunity to connect with the history, culture, and people of this vibrant region.

Chapter 7

Arts, Music, and Nightlife

Salta is a city where tradition and modernity harmoniously coexist, creating a vibrant cultural scene that captivates both locals and visitors. The region's arts, music, and nightlife are deeply influenced by its rich history and diverse cultural heritage, making Salta a destination where you can immerse yourself in both the old and the new. Whether you're drawn to the rhythms of traditional folklore music, the energy of the nightlife, or the creativity of local artists, Salta offers a dynamic cultural experience that leaves a lasting impression.

At the heart of Salta's cultural identity is traditional folklore music and dance, which is an integral part of the region's social fabric. Folklore music in Salta is characterized by its lively rhythms, emotive melodies, and poetic lyrics that often tell stories of love, nature, and the struggles of rural life. The most iconic instruments in Salteño folklore are the guitar, charango (a small stringed instrument), bombo (a large drum), and quena (a traditional Andean flute). The music is often accompanied by dance, with the zamba and chacarera being the most popular styles. The zamba is a graceful, romantic dance where couples move in a circular pattern, waving handkerchiefs as a symbol of courtship. The chacarera, on the other hand, is more spirited and lively, with dancers performing intricate footwork and playful movements. Folklore music and dance are not just performances in Salta; they are expressions of the region's soul, bringing people together in celebration of their shared heritage. You can experience this cultural tradition firsthand at peñas, which are traditional music venues where locals gather to listen to live performances, dance, and enjoy regional cuisine.

For those interested in the performing arts, Salta boasts a number of theaters and cultural centers that showcase a wide range of artistic expressions. The Teatro Provincial de Salta is the city's premier venue for classical music, opera, ballet, and theater. This elegant theater, with its neoclassical architecture and state-of-the-art facilities, hosts performances by both local and international artists, offering a diverse program that caters to all tastes. Another important cultural institution is the Casa de la Cultura, which serves as a hub for the arts in Salta. This historic building houses exhibition spaces, rehearsal rooms, and performance halls, and it regularly hosts events such as art exhibitions, film screenings, and theater productions. The Casa de la Cultura is also home to the Salta Philharmonic Orchestra, which performs concerts throughout the year. These theaters and cultural centers are vital to the city's cultural life, providing a platform for artists to share their work and for the community to engage with the arts.

When the sun sets, Salta comes alive with a vibrant nightlife scene that offers something for everyone. Salta's nightlife is a mix of traditional and contemporary, with options ranging from cozy bars to energetic clubs. The city's bars are perfect for those looking to unwind with a drink in a relaxed atmosphere. Many of the bars are located around the Plaza 9 de Julio and in the Balcarce district, which is the epicenter of Salta's nightlife. These establishments often feature live music, ranging from folklore to rock and jazz, creating an inviting ambiance where you can enjoy a cocktail or a glass of wine. For those who want to dance the night away, Salta's clubs offer a more upbeat experience, with DJs spinning everything from electronic music to Latin rhythms. The clubs usually start to fill up around midnight and stay open until the early hours of the morning, providing plenty of time to experience the city's vibrant party scene.

For music lovers, Salta is home to a variety of live music venues that showcase the region's rich musical heritage. One of the most popular venues is La Casona del Molino, a historic house turned peña where you can enjoy live folklore music in an intimate, traditional setting. The musicians at La Casona del Molino often play without amplification, creating an authentic, acoustic sound that resonates throughout the cozy space. Another great venue is Peña Balderrama, a legendary spot that has been a gathering place for folklore musicians and fans for decades. The atmosphere here is lively and festive, with patrons often joining in the dancing and singing. For those interested in more contemporary music, there are several venues in the Balcarce district that host live rock, jazz, and blues performances. These venues are popular with both locals and tourists, offering a chance to experience Salta's music scene in a more modern context.

Salta is also a city of festivals and events, with a calendar full of cultural celebrations that reflect the region's traditions and creativity. In 2024, several festivals will be taking place that offer visitors the opportunity to experience the best of Salta's arts, music, and culture. One of the most important events is the Fiesta Nacional de la Vendimia, held in March in Cafayate, which celebrates the grape harvest with wine tastings, folkloric performances, and a grand parade. Another major event is the Salta Jazz Festival, which takes place in November and features performances by both local and international jazz artists in various venues across the city. The festival has grown in popularity over the years, attracting jazz enthusiasts from all over Argentina and beyond. In addition to these annual events, Salta also hosts a number of smaller, community-driven festivals that highlight local traditions, such as the Fiesta del Milagro, which is a religious celebration in honor of the Virgin of the Miracle, the patron saint of Salta.

Salta's arts, music, and nightlife offer a rich and diverse cultural experience that reflects the city's unique blend of tradition and modernity. Whether you're drawn to the haunting melodies of folklore music, the creativity of local artists, or the energy of the nightlife, Salta has something to offer everyone. The city's cultural scene is a testament to the resilience and vibrancy of its people, who continue to celebrate their heritage while embracing new influences. As you explore Salta, you'll find that every corner of the city offers an opportunity to connect with its culture, whether through a live music performance, a visit to a gallery, or a night out on the town.

Chapter 8

Shopping in Salta

Salta is not only a destination for history, culture, and natural beauty, but also a vibrant hub for shopping, where visitors can discover unique local products, traditional crafts, and modern goods. The city and its surrounding areas offer a diverse shopping experience that blends the old with the new, providing travelers with ample opportunities to bring home a piece of Salta's rich heritage. From bustling artisan markets to sleek modern malls, here's an in-depth look at the shopping scene in Salta.

Artisan Markets and Handicrafts

One of the most rewarding aspects of shopping in Salta is the opportunity to explore its artisan markets, where local craftspeople showcase their skills and creativity. These markets are treasure troves of handmade goods, each reflecting the region's cultural diversity and artistic traditions. Among the most popular items are textiles, pottery, and jewelry, often crafted using techniques passed down through generations.

In these markets, you'll find beautifully woven ponchos, rugs, and blankets, made from the wool of llamas, alpacas, and sheep. The intricate patterns and vibrant colors of these textiles are deeply rooted in indigenous traditions, making them not only beautiful but also culturally significant. Each piece tells a story, with motifs that represent the landscapes, animals, and spiritual beliefs of the Andean peoples.

Pottery is another highlight of Salta's artisan markets. The clay used in these ceramics is sourced from the region's rich soils, and the designs often feature traditional motifs. Whether you're looking for decorative pieces or functional items like bowls and plates, the craftsmanship is sure to impress.

Jewelry is another craft that thrives in Salta, with artisans working in silver, an important metal in the region's history. From delicate earrings to bold statement pieces, the jewelry often incorporates local stones such as turquoise and malachite, adding a distinct Salteño touch.

The Mercado Artesanal, located in an old colonial building on Avenida San Martín, is one of the best places to explore these traditional crafts. Here, you can browse a wide range of products, meet the artisans themselves, and even watch as they work on their creations. The market is also a great place to learn about the different cultural influences that have shaped Salta's artisanal heritage, from indigenous to Spanish colonial.

Souvenirs and Local Products

Beyond the artisan markets, Salta offers a variety of other souvenirs and local products that make for perfect mementos of your visit. One of the most iconic items to bring home is a bottle of Torrontés wine. This aromatic white wine is a specialty of the region, known for its floral and fruity notes. Many shops in Salta sell Torrontés, often alongside other local wines, allowing you to take a taste of Salta's vineyards with you.

For food lovers, Salta is also famous for its delicious empanadas, and while you can't take these savory pastries home, you can find local cookbooks or traditional baking tools that make for unique and practical souvenirs. Packaged local delicacies like dried fruits, jams made from Andean berries, and artisanal chocolates are also popular choices.

Another distinctively Salteño product is the coca leaf, which has been used for centuries by the indigenous peoples of the Andes for its medicinal properties. While you'll find coca leaves and coca tea for sale throughout Salta, be sure to check the regulations regarding bringing these items back to your home country, as they may be restricted in some places.

Traditional musical instruments, such as the charango (a small Andean stringed instrument) and the quena (a traditional flute), also make for meaningful souvenirs, especially for those interested in South American music. Many shops in Salta specialize in these instruments, and some even offer lessons or demonstrations, giving you a deeper appreciation for the local musical traditions.

Best Shopping Streets

Salta's city center is home to several streets that are perfect for a leisurely shopping stroll. Calle Balcarce is one of the most popular, known not only for its lively nightlife but also for its eclectic mix of shops. Along this street, you'll find everything from high-end boutiques to small shops selling local crafts. It's a great place to shop for unique clothing, accessories, and home décor items, with many stores featuring products made by local designers.

Calle Caseros, which runs through the heart of Salta's historic center, is another excellent shopping destination. This street is lined with shops selling everything from fashion to souvenirs, and its central location makes it easy to combine a shopping trip with visits to nearby attractions like the Plaza 9 de Julio and the Cathedral. The architecture along Calle Caseros is also worth noting, with many beautifully preserved colonial buildings housing the shops.

For a more relaxed shopping experience, head to Paseo Güemes, a pedestrian-friendly area with a mix of cafes, shops, and galleries. This area is particularly popular in the evenings, when locals and tourists alike come to enjoy the atmosphere. The shops here tend to focus on arts and crafts, as well as gourmet food products, making it a great place to find unique gifts.

Modern Shopping Malls

While Salta is steeped in tradition, it also has a modern side, as evidenced by its shopping malls. Alto Noa Shopping is the city's largest and most modern mall, offering a wide range of stores that cater to all tastes and budgets. From international fashion brands to local retailers, Alto Noa has something for everyone. The mall also features a cinema, food court, and entertainment options, making it a popular destination for both shopping and leisure.

El Palacio Galerías is another modern shopping destination located in the city center. Housed in a historic building, this mall combines the charm of Salta's colonial past with contemporary shopping options. Here, you'll find a mix of fashion, electronics, and specialty stores, along with cafes where you can take a break from shopping.

For those interested in local fashion and design, the Galería Libertad is worth a visit. This boutique shopping center is home to a selection of stores that showcase the work of local designers, offering everything from clothing and accessories to home décor. It's a great place to discover Salta's burgeoning creative scene and to find one-of-a-kind items.

Where to Buy Traditional Gaucho Gear

The gaucho, Argentina's iconic cowboy, is an enduring symbol of the country's rural culture, and Salta is one of the best places to buy traditional gaucho gear. Whether you're looking for authentic leather boots, a wide-brimmed hat, or a finely crafted poncho, you'll find shops in Salta that specialize in these items.

One of the best places to shop for gaucho gear is the Feria Artesanal on Avenida San Martín. This market is known for its high-quality leather goods, including belts, boots, and saddles, all made using traditional methods. The craftsmanship is superb, and many of the items are handmade by local artisans.

For those looking for more specialized items, such as bombachas (traditional gaucho trousers) or silver knives known as facones, several stores in the city center cater specifically to gaucho culture. These shops often carry a range of products that reflect the lifestyle of the gauchos, from clothing and accessories to horse tack and riding gear.

Shopping for gaucho gear in Salta is not just about buying a product; it's about connecting with a way of life that has shaped the region's identity. Many of the items you'll find are not only functional but also steeped in tradition, making them meaningful souvenirs or gifts.

Salta's shopping scene offers a rich blend of the traditional and the contemporary, providing visitors with countless opportunities to take home a piece of the region's culture and creativity. Whether you're exploring artisan markets, browsing modern malls, or searching for authentic gaucho gear, you'll find that shopping in Salta is an experience as diverse and vibrant as the city itself.

Chapter 9

Day Trips and Excursions

Salta is not just a destination in itself but a gateway to some of the most breathtaking landscapes and cultural treasures in Argentina. Whether you're seeking adventure, cultural immersion, or a peaceful retreat in nature, the region surrounding Salta offers an array of day trips and excursions that will enrich your travel experience. Here's an in-depth look at some of the must-see destinations and experiences that await you just a short journey from Salta.

Exploring the Train to the Clouds (Tren a las Nubes)

The Train to the Clouds, or "Tren a las Nubes," is one of the most iconic railway journeys in the world and a highlight of any visit to Salta. This engineering marvel takes passengers on a breathtaking ride through the Andes, ascending to a staggering 4,200 meters (13,780 feet) above sea level. The journey begins in the city of Salta, with the train winding its way through the Lerma Valley before climbing into the rugged beauty of the Quebrada del Toro.

As the train snakes through the dramatic landscapes, passengers are treated to views of towering mountains, deep gorges, and remote villages where time seems to stand still. The journey is not just about the destination but the experience itself, with the train crossing 29 bridges, 21 tunnels, and 13 viaducts. The most famous of these is the La Polvorilla Viaduct, a 63-meter-high structure that gives the train its "clouds" moniker as it often appears to float above the mist.

The Train to the Clouds is more than just a scenic ride; it's an opportunity to connect with the region's rich history and culture. Onboard, local artisans sell traditional crafts, and guides share stories of the indigenous peoples and the construction of the railway. Whether you're a train enthusiast or simply looking for a unique adventure, this journey offers an unforgettable perspective on the majesty of the Andes.

Cachi: A Colonial Gem in the Mountains

Nestled in the shadow of the towering Nevado de Cachi, the town of Cachi is a charming colonial village that seems untouched by time. A day trip to Cachi is like stepping back into Argentina's colonial past, where cobblestone streets, adobe houses, and a serene pace of life create a perfect escape from the hustle and bustle of modern life.

The journey to Cachi from Salta is an adventure in itself, as you drive along the sinuous Cuesta del Obispo, a winding mountain road that offers spectacular views at every turn. The road climbs through the lush greenery of the Valle Encantado before reaching the desolate beauty of the high-altitude desert, where cacti stand sentinel against a backdrop of towering peaks.

Once in Cachi, you'll find plenty to explore. The town's main square, Plaza 9 de Julio, is the heart of the community, surrounded by historic buildings such as the 18th-century Church of San José, with its distinctive cactus wood ceiling. The Museo Arqueológico de Cachi is a must-visit, offering insights into the region's pre-Columbian history with its collection of artifacts from the indigenous Diaguita and Calchaquí cultures.

For those seeking outdoor adventure, the surrounding mountains offer excellent opportunities for hiking and exploring. The Cachi Adentro valley, with its fertile fields and orchards, is a particularly beautiful area to explore on foot or by bike. A visit to Cachi is a chance to immerse yourself in the tranquility and timeless beauty of Argentina's northwest.

Purmamarca and the Hill of Seven Colors

A visit to Purmamarca and its famous Hill of Seven Colors is a journey into a landscape that feels almost otherworldly. Located a few hours' drive from Salta, Purmamarca is a small village that has gained international fame for its stunning natural backdrop a multi-hued mountain that seems to change colors throughout the day.

The Hill of Seven Colors, or "Cerro de los Siete Colores," is the result of complex geological processes that have layered different minerals in the rock, creating vivid stripes of red, orange, yellow, green, and purple. The best time to see the hill is at sunrise or sunset when the colors are at their most vibrant, casting a surreal glow over the landscape.

Purmamarca itself is a charming village that retains much of its traditional character. The town's adobe houses, narrow streets, and central plaza, dominated by the centuries-old Iglesia de Santa Rosa de Lima, provide a glimpse into the region's colonial past.

The bustling handicraft market in the plaza is a great place to pick up locally made textiles, pottery, and jewelry.

Beyond the hill, the surrounding area offers plenty of opportunities for exploration. The Paseo de los Colorados is a short but rewarding hike that takes you through the striking red rock formations that encircle the village. For those willing to venture further, the nearby Salinas Grandes salt flats offer a stark contrast to the colorful hills and are an incredible place for photography.

The Wine Route: Vineyards and Tasting Tours

Salta's wine region, particularly around the town of Cafayate, is one of Argentina's most renowned, and a day trip along the Wine Route is a must for any oenophile. The high-altitude vineyards of the Calchaquí Valley produce some of the country's finest wines, particularly the aromatic Torrontés, which thrives in the region's unique climate.

A day trip to the wine region typically involves visiting several of the area's wineries, where you can tour the vineyards, learn about the winemaking process, and, of course, sample the wines. Many of the wineries are set against a stunning backdrop of mountains and vineyards, making for a truly picturesque experience.

Cafayate itself is a charming town with a relaxed atmosphere, where you can stroll through the central plaza, visit the local wine museum, or enjoy a leisurely lunch at one of the many restaurants offering regional specialties paired with local wines. Some wineries also offer bike tours, allowing you to pedal through the vineyards at your own pace, stopping to taste wines along the way.

For those with a deeper interest in wine, guided tours with local experts can provide insights into the region's unique terroir and the challenges of high-altitude viticulture. Whether you're a casual wine lover or a serious connoisseur, the Wine Route offers a day of indulgence and discovery in one of Argentina's most beautiful regions.

Adventure in the Quebrada del Toro

For those seeking an adrenaline rush and a chance to explore some of the most dramatic landscapes in the region, a day trip to the Quebrada del Toro is an ideal choice. This narrow canyon, carved by the Toro River, offers a rugged and remote wilderness that is perfect for outdoor adventures.

The Quebrada del Toro is known for its towering cliffs, dramatic rock formations, and the remnants of ancient civilizations that once inhabited the area. The canyon is also home to a variety of wildlife, including condors, guanacos, and vicuñas, making it a great destination for nature lovers.

Hiking is one of the most popular activities in the Quebrada del Toro, with several trails that offer stunning views of the canyon and the surrounding mountains. One of the most popular hikes is the

Camino del Inca, an ancient trail that was once part of the Inca road network. The trail offers a challenging but rewarding hike through rugged terrain, with the chance to see petroglyphs and other archaeological sites along the way.

For those interested in history and culture, the Quebrada del Toro also offers the opportunity to visit several small villages where you can learn about the region's indigenous heritage. The village of Tastil, for example, is home to the ruins of a pre-Inca settlement that once housed thousands of people. The site offers a fascinating glimpse into the lives of the people who once thrived in this harsh but beautiful landscape.

Whether you're seeking adventure, history, or simply the chance to explore one of the most stunning natural landscapes in Argentina, the Quebrada del Toro offers an unforgettable day trip from Salta.

These day trips and excursions offer a diverse array of experiences that showcase the best of what the Salta region has to offer. From the awe-inspiring Train to the Clouds to the serene beauty of Cachi and the vibrant landscapes of Purmamarca, each destination provides a unique window into the natural and cultural riches of northwest Argentina. Whether you're sipping wine in Cafayate or hiking through the Quebrada del Toro, these adventures will leave you with lasting memories of your time in Salta.

Chapter 10

Family Travel in Salta

Salta is an exceptional destination for families, offering a wide array of experiences that cater to travelers of all ages. Whether you're exploring historical sites, engaging in outdoor adventures, or immersing your children in cultural experiences, Salta has something for everyone. The city and its surrounding regions are not only rich in history and natural beauty but also welcoming and accessible to families. Here's an extensive guide to making the most of your family trip to Salta.

Kid-Friendly Attractions

Salta is home to numerous attractions that will capture the imagination of children and adults alike. The Museo de Arqueología de Alta Montaña (MAAM) is a must-visit for families. This museum, which houses the famous Inca mummies known as the Children of Llullaillaco, offers a fascinating glimpse into the region's ancient history. While the subject matter is profound, the museum presents it in a way that is accessible to children, with exhibits that are both informative and engaging. The interactive displays and clear explanations make it easy for young visitors to learn about the history and culture of the Andes.

For a more hands-on experience, the Teleférico San Bernardo is a thrilling way to see Salta from above. The cable car ride to the top of San Bernardo Hill offers breathtaking views of the city and the surrounding valleys, making it an exciting activity for children. At the summit, there's a park where kids can run around, and families can enjoy a picnic while taking in the panoramic vistas.

Another family-friendly attraction is the Tren a las Nubes (Train to the Clouds), one of the highest railways in the world. While the journey itself is awe-inspiring for adults, children will love the adventure of riding a train through the clouds. The onboard commentary is educational, making it a fun and informative experience for the whole family.

Family-Friendly Hotels

When traveling with children, finding the right accommodation is crucial to ensuring a comfortable and enjoyable stay. Salta offers a range of family-friendly hotels that cater to the needs of families with young children and teens. Many hotels in the city center provide amenities such as family suites, connecting rooms, and cribs, making them ideal for those traveling with kids.

One of the top choices for families is the Hotel del Virrey, a charming boutique hotel located in a beautifully restored colonial building. The hotel offers spacious family rooms and a central location that makes it easy to explore the city on foot. Another excellent option is the Alejandro I Hotel, which features larger rooms, an indoor pool, and a convenient location close to major attractions. The hotel's restaurant also offers a kid-friendly menu, making dining with little ones a breeze.

For families looking to stay outside the city center, Finca Valentina offers a unique experience. This boutique country house provides a peaceful retreat with spacious rooms, a large garden, and a pool, perfect for families who want to enjoy nature without straying too far from the city. The staff at Finca Valentina are known for their warm hospitality and can help arrange family-friendly activities in the surrounding area.

Outdoor Activities for All Ages

Salta's diverse landscapes make it an ideal destination for outdoor adventures that the whole family can enjoy. One of the most popular activities for families is exploring the Quebrada de Humahuaca, a UNESCO World Heritage site known for its stunning rock formations and colorful hills. The area offers several easy hiking trails that are suitable for children, allowing families to experience the beauty of the Andes at their own pace. The town of Purmamarca, with its famous Hill of Seven Colors, is particularly family-friendly, offering short walks and plenty of opportunities for photography.

For a more adventurous outing, families can head to the Salinas Grandes, the vast salt flats located a few hours from Salta. Kids will love the surreal landscape, where they can run around, take fun perspective photos, and learn about the unique environment. Many tour operators offer day trips to the salt flats, with guides who are experienced in working with families and can tailor the experience to the interests of children.

Horseback riding is another activity that is popular with families in Salta. Several estancias (ranches) around the city offer guided horseback riding tours that are suitable for all ages and experience levels. Riding through the valleys and mountains on horseback provides a unique way to explore the countryside and is sure to be a memorable experience for kids.

Cultural Experiences for Children

Introducing children to the rich culture of Salta is a rewarding experience that can enhance their understanding of Argentina's history and traditions. Many of Salta's cultural institutions offer programs and activities designed specifically for young visitors, making it easy to engage children in the local culture.

The Museo Pajcha, an ethnographic museum dedicated to the indigenous cultures of South America, is a fantastic place for families to learn about the diverse traditions and crafts of the region. The museum's exhibits are colorful and interactive, with plenty of hands-on activities that are perfect for children. Kids can learn about traditional textiles, pottery, and musical instruments, and even try their hand at some crafts.

During your stay in Salta, attending a peña is a must. These traditional folk music gatherings are a great way for families to experience local music and dance. Many peñas in Salta are family-friendly, with early evening shows that are suitable for children. Watching the dancers and musicians in traditional dress is sure to captivate young visitors, and some venues even offer dance lessons for kids.

Visiting local markets, such as the Mercado Artesanal, is another cultural experience that children will enjoy. The vibrant colors, the sounds of bargaining, and the opportunity to see artisans at work provide a sensory-rich experience that is both educational and entertaining. Children can watch as craftspeople create pottery, weave textiles, or carve wooden figures, giving them a deeper appreciation for the region's cultural heritage.

Tips for Traveling with Kids in Salta

Traveling with children in Salta can be a wonderful experience, but it's important to plan ahead to ensure a smooth and enjoyable trip. The first thing to consider is the altitude. Salta is located at a relatively high altitude, and some of the surrounding areas, such as the Train to the Clouds or the Quebrada de Humahuaca, are even higher. It's essential to allow time for your family to acclimatize, especially if you're coming from lower elevations. Make sure to keep your children well-hydrated, encourage them to rest if they feel tired, and avoid overly strenuous activities in the first few days.

When it comes to dining, Salta offers a wide range of options that cater to families. Many restaurants are used to accommodating children and will happily provide high chairs, kid-friendly menus, and even small portions of local dishes. Empanadas, a local specialty, are a great option for kids, as they are easy to eat and can be filled with a variety of ingredients that appeal to young palates.

Transportation in Salta is generally convenient for families. The city is walkable, and taxis are readily available and affordable. If you plan to explore the surrounding regions, renting a car can provide more flexibility, especially if you're traveling with young children who may need breaks during long drives. Many car rental agencies offer child seats, but it's a good idea to reserve them in advance.

Finally, packing for your trip to Salta should take into account the varied weather conditions. While the city itself has a relatively mild climate, the surrounding mountains can be much cooler, especially in the evenings. Be sure to bring layers, including hats and sunscreen, as the sun can be strong at higher altitudes. Comfortable walking shoes are also a must, especially if you plan to explore the natural landscapes.

Family travel in Salta offers a wealth of opportunities for exploration, adventure, and cultural immersion. Whether you're hiking through colorful canyons, learning about ancient civilizations, or simply enjoying the city's vibrant atmosphere, Salta provides a rich and rewarding experience for travelers of all ages. With its family-friendly accommodations, wide range of activities, and welcoming atmosphere, Salta is an ideal destination for your next family vacation.

Chapter 11

Sustainable Travel and Responsible Tourism

Salta's stunning landscapes, rich cultural heritage, and vibrant communities make it a top destination for travelers seeking authentic experiences. However, with the growing popularity of this region comes the responsibility to travel sustainably and practice responsible tourism. By making conscious choices about where to stay, what to do, and how to engage with local communities, visitors can help preserve Salta's natural beauty and cultural integrity for future generations. Here's a comprehensive guide to sustainable travel and responsible tourism in Salta.

Eco-Friendly Accommodations

Choosing eco-friendly accommodations is one of the most effective ways to minimize your environmental footprint while traveling in Salta. The region offers a growing number of lodgings that prioritize sustainability through eco-conscious practices, energy efficiency, and waste reduction. These accommodations are often located in or near natural settings, allowing guests to enjoy the beauty of the region while knowing that their stay is having a minimal impact on the environment.

Many eco-friendly hotels and lodges in Salta are built with sustainable materials and designed to harmonize with their surroundings. Solar power is often used for electricity and hot water, and water conservation practices such as rainwater harvesting and low-flow fixtures are common. Additionally, these establishments frequently incorporate organic gardens that supply fresh produce for their kitchens, reducing the need for transported goods and promoting farm-to-table dining.

For travelers who prefer a more immersive natural experience, eco-lodges located in the rural areas of Salta offer a unique opportunity to connect with the environment. These lodges typically emphasize the conservation of the surrounding ecosystem and often participate in local conservation efforts. By choosing to stay at an eco-lodge, visitors not only reduce their environmental impact but also contribute to the preservation of the region's biodiversity.

Supporting Local Communities

Responsible tourism is not only about protecting the environment but also about supporting the local communities that make a destination unique. In Salta, there are numerous ways to ensure that your travel dollars benefit the people who call this region home. One of the most direct ways to support local communities is by choosing to stay, eat, and shop at locally-owned businesses. This helps keep the money within the community, supporting local livelihoods and fostering economic development.

In addition to patronizing local businesses, consider participating in community-based tourism initiatives. These programs are designed to offer visitors an authentic cultural experience while providing economic benefits to local residents. In Salta, several indigenous communities offer homestays, guided tours, and cultural workshops, giving visitors a chance to learn about traditional ways of life, crafts, and customs. By engaging in these activities, travelers not only gain a deeper understanding of the region's culture but also contribute to the preservation of these traditions.

Another way to support local communities is by being mindful of the souvenirs you purchase. Look for items that are handmade by local artisans, using traditional methods and materials. This not only ensures that your purchases are ethically produced but also helps to sustain local crafts and cultural heritage. Markets such as the Mercado Artesanal in Salta are excellent places to find authentic, locally-made products.

Wildlife and Nature Conservation

Salta's diverse ecosystems are home to a wide variety of flora and fauna, many of which are unique to the region. However, these ecosystems are also fragile and vulnerable to the impacts of tourism. As a responsible traveler, it's important to be aware of the potential impact of your activities on local wildlife and natural habitats and to choose experiences that prioritize conservation.

When visiting natural areas, such as the Calchaquí Valleys or the Quebrada de Humahuaca, opt for guided tours led by knowledgeable local guides who are trained in environmental stewardship. These guides can offer insights into the local ecosystem and ensure that your visit does not disturb the wildlife or damage the environment. Additionally, some tour operators in Salta are actively involved in conservation efforts, such as reforestation projects or wildlife monitoring programs. By choosing these operators, you can directly support conservation initiatives during your visit.

It's also essential to follow the Leave No Trace principles when exploring natural areas. This means staying on designated trails, disposing of waste properly, and avoiding the collection of plants, animals, or other natural objects. If you encounter wildlife, observe from a distance and avoid feeding or interacting with the animals, as this can disrupt their natural behaviors and endanger their well-being.

Supporting conservation efforts can also extend to your choice of accommodations and activities. Some eco-lodges and tour operators contribute a portion of their profits to conservation projects, such as protecting endangered species or restoring native habitats. By staying at these establishments, you can contribute to the long-term preservation of Salta's natural heritage.

Sustainable Tour Operators

Choosing a sustainable tour operator is key to ensuring that your travel experiences in Salta are both environmentally responsible and culturally respectful. Sustainable tour operators prioritize eco-friendly practices, such as minimizing waste, reducing carbon emissions, and promoting environmental education. They also work closely with local communities, ensuring that tourism benefits are shared equitably and that cultural practices are respected.

When selecting a tour operator in Salta, look for certifications or memberships in organizations that promote sustainable tourism, such as the Global Sustainable Tourism Council (GSTC) or the Rainforest Alliance. These certifications indicate that the operator adheres to recognized sustainability standards and is committed to reducing its environmental impact.

Sustainable tour operators in Salta often offer small group tours, which not only reduce the environmental impact but also provide a more personalized and immersive experience. These tours typically focus on responsible wildlife viewing, cultural exchanges, and low-impact outdoor activities, such as hiking or cycling. By choosing a sustainable tour operator, you can enjoy the beauty and culture of Salta while knowing that your visit supports conservation and community development.

Tips for Reducing Your Environmental Impact

Even small actions can make a big difference when it comes to reducing your environmental impact while traveling in Salta. One of the simplest ways to travel sustainably is to minimize your use of single-use plastics. Bring a reusable water bottle, shopping bag, and utensils, and avoid products with excessive packaging. Many hotels and restaurants in

Salta are increasingly offering water refill stations and reducing their reliance on plastic, so it's easier than ever to avoid disposable items.

Another important consideration is your mode of transportation. While public transportation is not as extensive in Salta as in larger cities, there are still options for reducing your carbon footprint. Consider walking or cycling whenever possible, especially in the city center, where many attractions are within easy reach. For longer distances, choose shared transport options, such as buses or carpooling services, rather than private vehicles. If you do need to rent a car, look for companies that offer fuel-efficient or hybrid vehicles.

Energy conservation is another area where travelers can make a positive impact. Simple actions, such as turning off lights and air conditioning when not in use, can significantly reduce energy consumption. Additionally, many eco-friendly accommodations in Salta offer opportunities to learn about sustainable practices, such as solar energy or water conservation. Engaging with these initiatives can deepen your understanding of sustainability and inspire you to adopt similar practices at home.

When dining out, opt for restaurants that emphasize local, seasonal, and organic ingredients. This not only supports local farmers but also reduces the environmental impact associated with transporting food over long distances. In Salta, many restaurants take pride in offering dishes made from locally sourced ingredients, allowing you to enjoy the region's culinary traditions while supporting sustainable agriculture.

Lastly, consider offsetting the carbon emissions from your travel. Several organizations offer carbon offset programs that fund projects such as reforestation or renewable energy. By calculating the carbon footprint of your trip and purchasing offsets, you can mitigate the environmental impact of your travel to Salta.

Sustainable travel and responsible tourism are not just about minimizing harm; they are about making a positive impact on the places you visit. By choosing eco-friendly accommodations, supporting local communities, participating in conservation efforts, and traveling mindfully, you can help preserve the natural and cultural heritage of Salta for future generations. As more travelers embrace sustainable practices, we can collectively ensure that this beautiful region remains vibrant and thriving for years to come.

Chapter 12

Practical Information

When traveling to Salta, it's essential to be well-prepared with practical information that will ensure a smooth and enjoyable experience. From health and safety tips to understanding local customs and finding the best apps to assist you, this guide provides comprehensive details to help you navigate your journey with confidence.

Health and Safety Tips

Salta is generally a safe destination for travelers, but it's important to take basic precautions to ensure your health and safety during your stay. One of the first things to consider is the altitude. Salta city itself is situated at around 1,200 meters (3,937 feet) above sea level, but many of the surrounding areas, such as the Tren a las Nubes or the Quebrada de

Humahuaca, are at much higher altitudes. Altitude sickness can affect anyone, regardless of age or fitness level. Symptoms include headaches, dizziness, nausea, and shortness of breath. To minimize the risk, it's advisable to take it easy for the first few days, stay well-hydrated, and avoid alcohol. If you're planning to visit higher elevations, consider bringing medication for altitude sickness and consult your doctor before traveling.

When it comes to health care, Salta has several hospitals and clinics that provide good medical care. However, it's wise to have travel insurance that covers medical expenses and emergency evacuation, especially if you plan to engage in adventure activities like hiking or horseback riding in remote areas. Pharmacies are widely available in Salta, and many pharmacists speak English, making it easier to obtain over-the-counter medications.

Another health consideration is water quality. While tap water in Salta is generally safe to drink, many travelers prefer to drink bottled or filtered water, especially in more rural areas. It's also a good idea to carry hand sanitizer and wet wipes, as public restrooms may not always have soap and paper towels.

In terms of personal safety, Salta is relatively safe compared to larger cities in Argentina. Petty crime, such as pickpocketing and bag snatching, can occur, particularly in crowded areas or at tourist attractions. To protect your belongings, avoid displaying valuables, use a money belt or a crossbody bag, and be cautious in crowded places. It's also advisable to use registered taxis or ride-hailing apps rather than hailing a taxi on the street, especially at night.

Emergency Contacts

Being prepared with emergency contact information is crucial for any traveler. In Salta, the general emergency number is 911, which can be used to contact police, fire services, or medical emergencies. If you require medical assistance, Hospital San Bernardo and Clínica Güemes are two of the main hospitals in the city that cater to tourists.

For non-emergency medical advice or minor health issues, many pharmacies offer assistance and can recommend appropriate over-the-counter medications. In case of a lost passport or other travel documents, the nearest consulate or embassy should be contacted immediately. The Argentine government provides a 24-hour tourist assistance hotline (0800-555-5065), which can help with various issues, including lost documents or legal advice.

For travelers who do not speak Spanish, it may be useful to have a local contact or a translation app to assist in case of emergencies. It's also a good idea to keep a list of important numbers, such as your hotel, tour operator, and local contacts, easily accessible.

Language and Communication

Spanish is the official language of Argentina, and while many people in Salta speak some English, particularly in the tourism industry, it's helpful to know a few basic phrases in Spanish. This will not only make your trip smoother but will also be appreciated by the locals. Common greetings, polite expressions, and simple phrases like asking for directions or ordering food can go a long way in enhancing your travel experience.

If you're not fluent in Spanish, consider downloading a translation app such as Google Translate, which can help with both written and spoken communication. Many apps also offer offline capabilities, which can be useful in areas with limited internet access. Additionally, learning to read basic signage in Spanish, such as "salida" (exit) or "entrada" (entrance), can be helpful.

For staying connected, Wi-Fi is widely available in Salta, especially in hotels, cafes, and restaurants.

However, if you need constant access to the internet or want to avoid high roaming charges, consider purchasing a local SIM card. The main mobile carriers in Argentina are Movistar, Claro, and Personal, all of which offer prepaid SIM cards with data plans. These can be easily purchased at the airport, mobile stores, or kiosks throughout the city.

Currency, Banking, and ATMs

The official currency in Argentina is the Argentine peso (ARS). In Salta, cash is still widely used, particularly in smaller shops, markets, and rural areas. While many hotels, restaurants, and larger stores accept credit cards, it's advisable to carry some cash for smaller transactions. ATMs are readily available in the city, but they often have withdrawal limits, and some charge high fees for foreign cards. It's a good idea to withdraw larger amounts at once to minimize fees.

Currency exchange services are available at banks, official exchange offices (casas de cambio), and some hotels. It's recommended to exchange money at official establishments rather than on the street to avoid counterfeit bills. Keep in mind that U.S. dollars are widely accepted in Argentina, particularly in tourist areas, and some businesses may even offer a better exchange rate if you pay in dollars.

When using credit or debit cards, be aware that some places may add a surcharge for card payments, especially for international cards. It's also important to notify your bank before traveling to avoid any issues with card transactions abroad. If you plan to use a credit card frequently, choose one that doesn't charge foreign transaction fees.

Useful Apps for Travelers

Traveling in Salta can be made easier and more enjoyable with the use of a few key apps. For navigation, Google Maps is an invaluable tool for finding your way around the city and planning day trips. The app also provides information on public transportation routes, walking directions, and the location of nearby attractions, restaurants, and services.

For language assistance, Google Translate is a popular choice, offering translation for text, speech, and even images. The app's offline mode is especially useful in areas with limited connectivity. Duolingo is another app worth considering if you want to brush up on your Spanish before or during your trip.

When it comes to transportation, ride-hailing apps like Uber and Cabify are available in Salta and can be a convenient way to get around, especially if you prefer not to use local taxis. Both apps allow you to see the fare upfront, choose your payment method, and track your ride in real-time.

For currency conversion, XE Currency is a reliable app that provides up-to-date exchange rates and allows you to track multiple currencies. This is particularly useful when budgeting for your trip or when exchanging money.

Lastly, to stay informed about the weather, download an app like AccuWeather or The Weather Channel. These apps provide detailed forecasts, including temperature, precipitation, and wind conditions, helping you plan your activities and pack appropriately.

Important Local Customs and Etiquette

Understanding and respecting local customs and etiquette is key to having a positive and culturally enriching experience in Salta. Argentinians are known for their warmth and hospitality, and social interactions are often more informal and friendly compared to other cultures. When greeting someone, a handshake or a kiss on the cheek is common, even when meeting someone for the first time. It's customary to kiss on the right cheek, and this applies to both men and women.

When dining out, it's important to note that dinner is typically served later in the evening, often starting around 9:00 PM or later. If you're invited to a local's home, it's polite to bring a small gift, such as wine or sweets, and to compliment the host on the meal. Table manners are similar to those in Europe, with the fork held in the left hand and the knife in the right. It's also common to linger at the table after a meal, enjoying conversation over coffee or a digestif.

Tipping is customary in Salta, particularly in restaurants. The standard tip is around 10% of the bill, although some people may leave slightly more for excellent service. It's also customary to tip hotel staff, tour guides, and taxi drivers, although the amounts are typically smaller.

When visiting religious sites, such as churches or shrines, dress modestly and be respectful of those who are there to worship. Photography may be restricted in some areas, so it's best to ask for permission before taking pictures.

Finally, it's important to be mindful of environmental practices while in Salta. Littering is frowned upon, and many locals take pride in keeping their natural surroundings clean. Participate in this by disposing of waste properly and recycling where possible. By following these customs and etiquette, you'll not only show respect for the local culture but also enhance your own experience in Salta.

This practical information is designed to help you navigate Salta with ease, allowing you to focus on enjoying everything this beautiful region has to offer. Whether you're hiking in the Andes, exploring colonial towns, or immersing yourself in the local culture, being well-prepared will ensure a memorable and rewarding journey.

Chapter 13

Salta in 2024: What's New?

In 2024, Salta is experiencing an exciting transformation, blending its rich cultural heritage with modern developments that make it an even more attractive destination for travelers. The year brings a mix of new attractions, events, and developments that are sure to captivate visitors, as well as insider tips to enhance the travel experience.

Salta has always been known for its colonial architecture, vibrant cultural scene, and breathtaking landscapes, but 2024 introduces several new attractions that add to its charm. One of the most anticipated additions is the expansion of the Museo de Arqueología de Alta Montaña (MAAM), which is famous for housing the well-preserved Inca mummies known as the

"Children of Llullaillaco." The museum has unveiled new exhibits that delve deeper into the region's pre-Columbian history, offering interactive displays and digital reconstructions that make the ancient past come alive for visitors. Another noteworthy addition is the Salta Wine Experience, an immersive attraction that celebrates the province's renowned wine industry. Located on the outskirts of the city, this new center offers wine-tasting sessions, vineyard tours, and educational workshops on the winemaking process, providing a comprehensive introduction to the region's celebrated Torrontés wines.

Salta's event calendar for 2024 is packed with new and returning favorites. The Festival Internacional de la Cultura Andina is set to be a major highlight, bringing together artists, musicians, and performers from across the Andean region. This festival, held in September, is a vibrant showcase of indigenous culture, with traditional music, dance, and handicrafts taking center stage. Additionally, the city will host the first Salta Film Festival, focusing on Latin American cinema. This event is expected to attract filmmakers and cinephiles from around the world, offering screenings, workshops, and discussions that highlight the region's growing film industry. For those interested in the region's natural beauty, the Andean Wildlife Photography Exhibit is a must-see. This traveling exhibit, which will be in Salta from June through August, features stunning images of the region's diverse wildlife, captured by some of South America's most talented photographers.

Upcoming developments in Salta reflect the city's ongoing commitment to enhancing its appeal while preserving its unique character. The expansion of the city's public transportation network is one such development. A new tram line connecting the city center with the surrounding neighborhoods and key tourist sites is slated for completion by the end of 2024. This eco-friendly transportation option will make it easier for visitors to explore Salta without relying on cars, reducing traffic congestion and minimizing the environmental impact of tourism. Furthermore, the city's historic center is undergoing a significant restoration project. Several of Salta's iconic colonial buildings are being restored to their former glory, with efforts to maintain the architectural integrity of these structures while integrating modern amenities. This project is part of a broader initiative to secure Salta's designation as a UNESCO World Heritage Site, a status that would recognize its cultural and historical significance on a global scale.

For travelers heading to Salta in 2024, there are several insider tips that can enhance the experience. First, it's worth noting that Salta is becoming a year-round destination, thanks to the mild climate and the growing number of indoor attractions and events. However, visiting during the shoulder seasons—April to May and September to October—offers the advantage of fewer crowds and lower prices, while still enjoying pleasant weather.

Additionally, food lovers should take advantage of the growing number of peñas (traditional folk music clubs) that offer not just live music but also authentic Salteño cuisine. These venues are the perfect place to sample regional specialties like empanadas salteñas and locro, accompanied by live zamba or chacarera performances.

Another insider tip is to explore beyond the city. While Salta itself has plenty to offer, the surrounding region is dotted with hidden gems. The small village of Cachi, for instance, is a lesser-known destination that provides a serene escape with its whitewashed adobe buildings, cobblestone streets, and panoramic views of the Andes. Meanwhile, the Quebrada de las Flechas, a stunning geological formation located along the Ruta 40, is perfect for those seeking adventure and natural beauty. Guided tours that include both destinations are increasingly popular, providing a more intimate experience of Salta's diverse landscapes.

2024 is shaping up to be a pivotal year for Salta, with new attractions, events, and developments that promise to enhance its status as a must-visit destination in Argentina. Whether exploring the city's rich cultural offerings or venturing into the stunning Andean countryside, travelers will find plenty to discover and enjoy.

Chapter 14

Useful Resources

For travelers planning a trip to Salta in 2024, having access to useful resources can significantly enhance the experience. Whether you're looking for cinematic inspiration, seeking detailed information online, or needing reliable local contacts and tour operators, this section will provide you with everything you need to make the most of your visit to this fascinating region.

One of the best ways to immerse yourself in the culture and landscape of Salta before your trip is through film. Several movies have captured the essence of the region, offering a visual journey that can deepen your appreciation of Salta's unique beauty. One highly recommended film is "Aballay, el hombre sin miedo" (Aballay, the Man Without

Fear), directed by Fernando Spiner. This 2010 Argentine drama, set in the rugged landscapes of northwest Argentina, including Salta, tells the story of a gaucho who renounces violence after a life-altering encounter. The film's stunning cinematography showcases the dramatic scenery of the region, making it a compelling watch for those interested in the intersection of myth, history, and the natural environment. Another notable film is "La Ciénaga" (The Swamp), directed by Lucrecia Martel. While not explicitly set in Salta, this critically acclaimed film is deeply rooted in the Argentine northwest, reflecting the social and cultural dynamics of the region. Martel, who hails from Salta, uses the suffocating heat and rural setting to explore the tensions and dysfunctions within a bourgeois family, providing a poignant commentary on life in the region.

For travelers seeking more in-depth information about Salta, a wealth of websites and blogs are dedicated to exploring the region's attractions, culture, and travel tips. One essential resource is Salta Turismo (www.turismosalta.gov.ar), the official tourism website for the province. This site offers comprehensive information on accommodations, events, and attractions, along with practical details on transportation and weather. It's an invaluable starting point for planning your trip, with regularly updated content and official recommendations. Another excellent online resource is All About Salta (www.allaboutsalta.com), a blog run by a local expat who shares insider tips, travel itineraries, and personal experiences exploring Salta and its surroundings. The blog is particularly useful for discovering off-the-beaten-path destinations and lesser-known activities that might not be covered in traditional travel guides. Additionally, the website Salta Argentina (www.salta-argentina.com) is a great resource for learning more about the cultural and historical aspects of the region, with articles on local customs, festivals, and the rich indigenous heritage of Salta.

When it comes to organizing your trip, working with a reputable travel agency or tour operator can make all the difference. Salta is home to several well-established agencies that offer a range of services, from guided tours to customized travel packages. One of the most recommended is Say Hueque (www.sayhueque.com), a travel company that specializes in tailor-made itineraries throughout Argentina, including Salta. They offer a variety of tours, from wine-tasting excursions in the Calchaquí Valleys to adventure trips through the Andes, all designed to provide an authentic experience of the region. Another trusted operator is Tangol (www.tangol.com), known for their extensive range of tours in northern Argentina. Their offerings include everything from half-day city tours of Salta to multi-day treks in the Quebrada de Humahuaca, with knowledgeable guides who bring the region's history and culture to life. For those interested in eco-friendly travel,Sayta Cabalgatas(www.sayta.com.ar) is a standout choice.

This family-run business offers horseback riding tours through the stunning landscapes around Salta, with a strong focus on sustainable tourism practices.

Having reliable local contacts and access to tourist information centers is essential for navigating Salta and making the most of your visit. The main tourist information center in Salta is located at Caseros 711, right in the heart of the city. Here, you can pick up maps, brochures, and get advice from knowledgeable staff who can assist with everything from booking tours to finding the best restaurants. The staff can also provide information on current events and festivals, ensuring that you don't miss out on any of the region's cultural highlights. Additionally, there are smaller information centers located at key tourist sites, such as the Museo de Arqueología de Alta Montaña and the Teleférico San Bernardo, where you can obtain site-specific information and purchase tickets for local attractions.

For more personalized assistance, consider contacting Salta's Office of Tourism directly. They can be reached via phone or email and offer services in multiple languages, including English. This office is an invaluable resource for travelers who may need assistance with more complex travel arrangements or who have specific questions about their itinerary. Local hotels and guesthouses often have connections with reliable guides and drivers, and many can arrange private tours or transportation on request, making them another useful resource for visitors.

Whether you're preparing for your trip by watching films that capture the spirit of Salta, browsing blogs and websites for insider tips, booking tours with trusted operators, or seeking assistance from local contacts, these resources will help you to experience the best that Salta has to offer in 2024. With a little planning and the right information, your journey to this remarkable region will be both enriching and unforgettable.

Chapter 15

Final Thoughts

As you prepare to embark on your journey to Salta in 2024, it's essential to consider how to make the most of your trip, how to leave a positive impact on the places you visit, and what memories you will cherish long after your adventure ends. This region, with its stunning landscapes, rich cultural heritage, and warm hospitality, offers an experience that is both profound and unforgettable.

To truly make the most of your trip to Salta, immerse yourself in everything the region has to offer. Start by exploring the city's historic center, where colonial architecture and vibrant plazas paint a picture of Salta's rich past. Take your time wandering through the cobblestone streets, visiting landmarks like the Catedral Basílica de Salta and the Cabildo Histórico. Don't rush; allow yourself to absorb the atmosphere and appreciate the intricate details of these historic sites. When planning your itinerary, consider balancing your time between cultural activities and outdoor adventures. Salta is known for its incredible landscapes, from the dramatic rock formations of Quebrada de las Conchas to the high-altitude vineyards of Cafayate. Plan at least one excursion into the countryside, whether it's a trek through the Quebrada de Humahuaca, a visit to the salt flats at Salinas Grandes, or a scenic drive along the Ruta 40. These experiences will give you a deeper connection to the land and a greater understanding of the natural beauty that defines this region.

Another aspect of making the most of your trip involves connecting with the local culture. Salta's cultural identity is deeply rooted in its indigenous heritage, colonial history, and the traditions of its people. Attend a peña, a traditional folk music gathering, where you can enjoy live music, dance, and authentic Salteño cuisine. Engaging with locals, whether through organized tours or casual conversations, will enrich your experience and provide insights that you won't find in guidebooks. Learn a few phrases in Spanish, try the local dishes like empanadas salteñas and humita en chala, and participate in local customs and festivals. These small efforts to engage with the culture will deepen your appreciation of Salta and create lasting memories.

Leaving a positive impact during your visit to Salta is an important consideration, especially as tourism continues to grow in the region. One way to do this is by practicing sustainable tourism. Choose eco-friendly accommodations that prioritize environmental conservation and support local communities. Many hotels and lodges in Salta are committed to sustainability, from reducing water and energy consumption to sourcing food locally. When booking tours, opt for operators that follow ethical practices, such as limiting group sizes, minimizing environmental impact, and respecting local wildlife and habitats. Another way to leave a positive impact is by supporting local businesses. Whether you're dining at a family-owned restaurant, buying handicrafts from an artisan market, or booking a tour with a local guide, your spending directly benefits the community and helps to preserve the cultural heritage of the region. Additionally, be mindful of your environmental footprint. Salta's natural landscapes are delicate, so take care to follow Leave No Trace principles. Dispose of waste properly, avoid disturbing wildlife, and stick to marked trails when hiking. These small actions contribute to the preservation of Salta's beauty for future generations.

As your journey through Salta comes to an end, you'll want to take home memories that capture the essence of your experience. While photographs are an obvious choice, consider collecting items that reflect the region's culture and traditions. A bottle of Torrontés wine from the Cafayate region makes for a perfect souvenir, offering a taste of Salta's unique terroir that you can enjoy long after your trip. Handcrafted items, such as woven textiles, pottery, or silver jewelry, are also meaningful mementos that support local artisans and celebrate the region's rich artistic heritage. If you're looking for a more personal keepsake, consider a piece of pachamama art, which is often inspired by indigenous beliefs and the natural world. These works of art, whether they take the form of paintings, sculptures, or crafts, carry with them the spiritual connection that many locals have with the land. Beyond physical items, the most valuable memories you'll take home are the experiences and connections you've made. The conversations with locals, the flavors of traditional dishes, the awe-inspiring landscapes, and the sounds of folk music—all these elements will stay with you long after you've left Salta.

In conclusion, a trip to Salta in 2024 offers a unique opportunity to explore one of Argentina's most captivating regions. By immersing yourself in the culture, practicing sustainable tourism, and bringing home meaningful memories, you'll ensure that your experience is not only enjoyable but also impactful. Salta has a way of leaving an indelible mark on those who visit, and with the right approach, your journey will be one of discovery, connection, and lasting memories.

Printed in Great Britain
by Amazon

60649505R00077